backbone

m.k.

i would like to give special thanks to my designer, Austin, for his patience and knowledge to help bring my vision to life.

i would also like to show my greatest gratitude to my dear friend, Eduardo, for serving as a mentor and educator throughout the creation of this project.

there is no organization, no story line, no beginning to end, and no happy ending. some days i feel it in my neck, and some days i feel it running down my whole entire spine. that is why i speak of the backbone. it covers every area that i feel the aches and the pains; it is where body and mind align; it is the strongest, yet the weakest part of my body. my weaknesses plant the seeds and my strengths show them the light. it is when i feel no pain at all that i am reminded of growth, and yet another bud on my vertebrae that has bloomed. my backbone is a reminder of where i have been, where i am now, and where i want to be; a reminder of what i have felt, what i am feeling, and what i want to feel. i sense it, i nurture it, and i bloom—this is how i grow. here is to my long nights, shared with you through short excerpts of an ongoing journey to self-love and healing. i hope to impact you in some way. or even better, help you plant a new seed along your garden. feel that pinched nerve in the crevice of your backbone or that knot building up in your neck

// you can release it here

here is a safe place for you and i
where there are no secrets and no judgements
allow yourself to be vulnerable amongst these words
because it is okay to feel
and it is always time to heal and to grow
it is either the season to plant
or the season to bloom
plant the seeds when you feel the timing is right
and trust the cycle
this is one seed, one bud
i have planted amongst my vertebrae
and there is plenty of ground to plant more
i plan on having my roots reach even the deepest soil
the kind of soil that people do not speak of
the kind that deserves to be spoken of
this is for the ones who remain quiet
and for me, who will remain quiet no more

i have found the cure
for my writer's block at last
it was when i learned
to be inspired by everything
every place, every face
and every piece of my broken heart

trauma
self-pity
depression
anxiety
anger

i have turned to art
all through the simplicity of words
who knew these words of mine
would find the tip of my tongue again
something i thought i lost
so, here i am
and i am planning on staying awhile
i hope you do, too

my words now have a home
and there is plenty of room for you

// get cozy as i take you through a journey of aches and
pains, as well as love and healing

{THESE ARE THE THINGS THAT HAVE BEEN PLACED AMONGST MY BACKBONE}

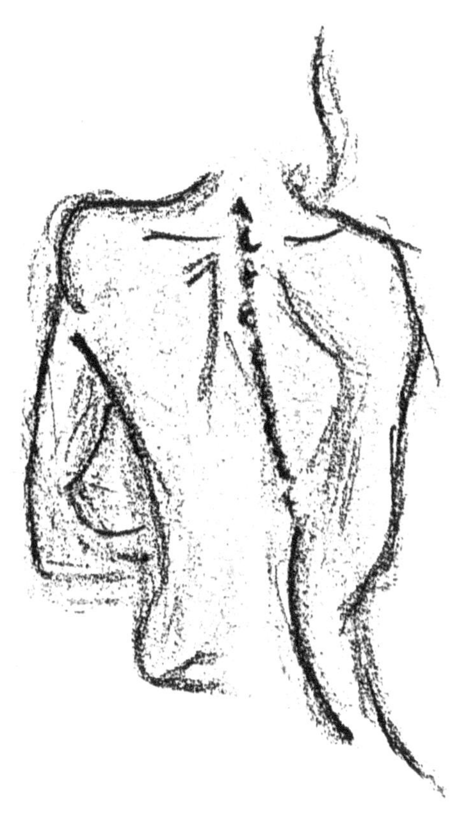

{MY BLOOD, SWEAT, AND TEARS}

he said i was too sensitive
so i made sure to leave my tears
scattered amongst these pages
but they are dry now
that is the beauty of pain
it comes and goes
when it comes
i break
when it goes
i build,
wipe my tears
and become stronger than before
each and every time

// make these pages your tissue, too

{INNOCENCE}

as she looked down at her sobbing wet
and crinkled tissues,
they reminded her of a pure flower
like a pure, delicate child she once knew

the world had not taken her
beneath her feet yet,
for she was too young to know
the trap she was getting herself into

growing up

this story goes way back
before the divorce, before the abuse,
and before she became a victim of anxiety

she prays
to something bigger than herself,
wishing she could know that little girl again

someday,
she says

as she looks back down at those sobbing wet
and crinkled tissues once more

// live your life the way your younger
self would want you to

2

{MOVE ON}

time moves fast
when you're living in the past

while you dwell and ache,
you are not progressing
as you remain still,
everything else does not

cars are passing,
seasons are changing
the clock still ticks and goes,
and so do opportunities

{MENTAL ILLNESS}

drowning is a lot like
what an anxiety attack feels like

i want you to imagine yourself slowly entering an ocean,
sinking deeper and deeper

your mind is racing, your vision is foggy
you go to take a breathe and swallow,
but you choke at the fear of the unknown
in which you are entering

as you continue sinking deeper and deeper
you allow the anxiety to take over,
knowing that trying to fight it
will just make you drown quicker

your heart is racing, your stomach is aching
you're sweating, you're shivering
till you eventually lose all feeling completely

by this time you've lost hope, hitting rock bottom
as you lay there on the ocean floor,
there is no one in sight

it is just you, the ocean,
and your chronic anxiety that has taken control

// educate yourself on mental illness.
it's everywhere,
and so many people are drowning in it

{THE AFTER STORM}

your goals ahead may seem blurry,
unachievable

but i can promise you this

once you get past the rain,
the storm,
the blur,

you will learn to
love dancing in the rain,
chasing the storm,
and sitting back to watch for the rainbow

the rainbow that always shines through

{HOMEBODY}

your body is your home
the only home you can always come home to,
the only lover that can always be faithful,
and the only warm bed you can always crawl into

your body;

the only thing you have complete control of
so decorate it with pretty things,
talk nice to it,
and make it comfy

// become a homebody of your own body

the ocean, The Great Unknown, is the world's grace. we are all sinking in it, reaching for God Almighty's hand; however, we aren't meeting halfway. for God to take our hand and pull us out of our anxieties, we must first be in reachable distance. for the Lord said in the book of Peter, "Cast all your anxiety on Him because he cares for you." as we stand on the shore casting our fishing poles into the water, we aren't catching anything. as the same goes for the Lord, He can't catch any fish (us) without trusting in Him to reel us in. let us humble ourselves, for He is healing your past, holding your hand in the present, and planning your future all at the same time. for only God is sovereign. because of this great power that only He holds, let us trust in Him with our whole heart. we must not stress, for God has created different seasons for different reasons. if we were to try to plant in the middle of winter, the crops would not survive. as goes for us, we must sense the season and choose (because God gives us free will) to either go with the current where it is easy and unrewarding, or we can go against the current and tackle life coming at us faster than we think we can handle. but i promise you, after you overcome these currents throughout the seasons, the reward is priceless—Heaven

// this one is for the believers and the non-believers. and for the non-believers, i challenge you to try and believe in something higher than yourself. we cannot do it on our own

{BAD HABITS}

i have this unhealthy habit
of clinging to things that give me life

even if those things
are only temporary

// you became my bad habit

{NERVES}

my head,
tells me everything i am not

my eyes,
release rivers of tears onto my pillow at night

my ears,
hear the verbal abuse

my nose,
smells the depressants i use to take away the pain

my mouth,
tastes the lips of disrespectful men

my heart,
wants what it cannot have

my hands,
never stop shaking

my stomach,
never stops aching

between my legs,
craves anything that gives me attention

and everything below my legs,
i can no longer feel

{MIND GAMES}

you bankrupt me
like a game of Monopoly

where you're always the player
and i'm always the game

// but i was made for the game

{FROSTBITE}

you're cold to the touch,
yet you turn me rosy

you're blinding to the eye,
but have this sparkle about you
that keeps me staring

you're dangerous,
yet i always find myself
wishing for more

you're gone so quick,
but leave me dreaming
of your return

// he reminded me of snow

{SOCIETY'S STANDARDS}

the male species: one of dominance, pride, and lust
the female species: one of obeying, insecurity, and fragility

but who created this system,
where men cannot cry

and women are expected
to shatter like glass amongst the feet of the male?

{SCARS}

crevices
cracks
cuts

people call them
open wounds

i call them possibilities
for light to shine through

and to close them up
like scars

after all,
this is how scars are formed;
from

the hurt
the pain
and the healing

// let the light in

{THANKFUL}

i thank my trauma everyday
for without it i'd be a conformist of society

{POLAR OPPOSITES}

you are the fire
and i am the water

the perfect balance
they say

but you scorch me with your anger
and i drown you with my sorrows

{UTOPIA}

i dream of a place;
a new environment surrounded by unfamiliar,
yet kind faces

a place where all people share the same vision;
one of beauty and chaos

you see,
the people here feed on the chaos
rather than letting it burn their city to ashes

for it is the trauma
that makes this place so beautiful

the buildings are structured with hope,
the streets are paved with ambition,
and the trees carry the dreams that come true here

{MALNUTRITION}

you came into my life
and stripped me clean

i was left dehydrated,
malnourished

it's like my body knew
i deserved to starve

{FAIRYTALES}

my upcoming was nothing like a fairytale

i was shown that love was
screaming
slamming of doors
punching
shoving
touching someone other than your wife;
what a joke of love

this is why your love is unreal

you show me that love can be
soft words before bed
holding doors open
unbroken promises
pulling me in slowly
respecting this body that i give to you;
what a dream come true

// my happy ending

{HIGH-MAINTENANCE}

my mind is filled with dreams;
help them come true

my eyes drown me in tears;
hold me afloat

my mouth salivates for my anti-depressants;
be my medicine

my lips are raw from anxious habits;
kiss me slowly

my heart is a garden of wilting flowers;
water me

my stomach is hungry for a love like yours;
feed me

my urges are not of my roots;
teach me resistance

my legs cannot hold my anxiety;
help me carry the weight

my body is protected by a guard i have built;
break it and soften me

// to the men who still want me

{SPEECHLESS}

you take the words right out of my mouth
and leave me with nothing but this blank page

...

{MY FOREVER HOME}

what is better than one unstable structure
is two unstable structures

two for balance
two for leaning on
two for reconstruction

you were the fixer upper i needed

we balance with our differences
we lean on but never depend on
and we continue to reconstruct the broken pieces

the broken pieces
a home will always have

no home is perfect
but ours feels like the one we are meant to be in

to grow in
and to live in

forever,
and ever

{FALLING IN LOVE}

you run electricity through my veins,
and ignited this fire in my soul

if we are not careful,
we could burn forests down, love

{CRAVINGS}

i am always craving more

more pleasure
more attention
more love

i am like an addict
with withdrawals of self-love,
for it has been gone for so long

i crave someone
to fulfill all of these urges

// i crave myself

{SURVIVOR}

i have returned from battle,
battle against myself

i shed
blood,
sweat,
tears,
and people

to the people that fought by my side
and the ones that did not

thank you

for the memories,
the lessons,
and the growth

without you,
i could not have won the war

{HONOR}

i am so damn proud to be a woman;
a concept i once felt humiliated of
with the periods and the expectations of perfection
i was taught that the male makes all dominant decisions,
that women cannot be sexual beings without being shamed,
and that i should live in fear of speaking my mind
because it would not be justified nor heard
but we carry life,
human life; a pure miracle
we carry a human being inside of our bodies for nine months
nine months filled with pains,
aches,
abnormal cravings,
hormonal imbalances,
and distortions of the body,
yet we are labeled weak
to all you women, we must not be ashamed
love your body,
love your ideas,
love your thoughts,
and love your goals;
you are beautiful,
you are heard,
you are worthy,
and you are capable
you owe no one anything, especially the male
so let us stand together,
for without us there is no future

// because we are the future

{SEASONAL DEPRESSION}

cloudy days,
they test me to find the sunshine within myself

{ROSES}

they grow strong
when you cut all the dead stuff off of them

{MAKING LOVE}

i want to be kissed like the sun
i want to be guided like the moon during my darkest hours

so lay me down like the moon does the sun
and light me up like the stars do the sky

{01.15.18}

we were intoxicated last night;
intoxicated off bittersweet wine

we finished two bottles,
two trophies of mine

i crave another sip,
and i'm not just talking about the wine

{OPEN LETTER TO ANXIETY}

hello my dear old friend,

i have not spoken of you in months, but i just wanted to say thank you. as i continue to overthink every second of my waking hours, i see art; not toxicity. i create; not destroy. i look at a flower and see myself. i see myself as a bud, where at that point i refused to open up. i felt safer inside each petal, closed off from a world where i did not feel understood. i see myself as the petals, slowly opening up one by one. each petal represents a voice that i overcame and defeated. i now do not see, but am a bloomed, radiant flower. my trauma and you as the aftermath are my biggest critics, my inspiration, my drive, my roots. i have learned to not be ashamed of you, but to water and nourish the roots that got me here. i am an exotic flower; a wildflower. and i am never letting you pull me from the soil i have created for myself. a soil of acceptance and drive to make a difference.

{INSTABILITY}

i am radioactive
i am a nuclear bomb waiting to go off

get away while you can,
before your atoms become unstable like mine

{DRAMATIC}

my anxiety gets thrilled
when i get into a relationship;

an opportunity for it to be the producer
of another overrated chick flick of my life

{MUTUAL EFFORT}

you will never be loved more deeply
than by the girl who has fought like hell
to know the love she deserves

if you can give that kind of love to her

you will never feel disloyalty
unworthy
unloved

// you must give to receive in any relationship

{MY MASTERPIECE}

i am an artist
and you are my canvas

the blank slate i have been waiting for
the new beginning i have been yearning for

so let us make art of this
and display it for everyone to see, baby

// art in the making

{SERENITY}

there is something so serene
about the moon taking over the sky
(nighttime)

we become silent and restful,
but there are some things that never sleep
(the city)

with its vibrant lights
and restless nights,
the city never dies

i want to feel alive

i want to see the city
when it is a ghost town;

where the allies are filled with nothing
but my own shadow,

where my eyes gleam
of the street lights and the stars,

and where we,
just you and i,

can dance the night away

{11:53PM}

my chest is tight
and filled with despite

my heart is beating fast
nothing will ever last

my hands are clammy and sweaty
thinking of you being with someone other than me

// i have been fighting with my demons tonight

{BROKEN ROOTS}

i am trying to build my home, myself,
but it never remains standing

there are cracks in the foundation,
and there will always be cracks

there will always be that echo
from the lack of love,

those torn pages
of the wedding scrapbook,

and rings and bands
of a broken promise in my hope chest

but then i came across you
during the process of renovating

you've started to fill
the cracks,

you create music that fills
every vacant space,

you are the new beginning
of my broken story,

and the promise
i have been waiting for

// you are home

{BRAINSTORMING}

just like a lightbulb,

we have our positive charges
and our negative charges

without both,
there cannot be light

without our positive attributes,
we would not have bright ideas;

without our negative attributes,
we would not shine apart from everyone else

once we charge
and balance,

we ignite;
we light up the sky;
we dance

at this point,

there is no darkness;
no demons;
and no one that can stop us and our light

{LIFE IS WORTH LIVING}

every day is a fight for my life

a fight
to breathe with a suffocating mind,
to get out of bed in the morning,
to go to work,
to feed my body with healthy habits,
to find words that do not push the ones i love away,
and to find the will to live

depression and anxiety try to kill me every day

but today and all the days that follow
i'll continue to find that will to live
and the things worth living for

// for all the fighters reading,
make a list of things worth living for and hold them tight

{ACCEPTANCE}

i will always be
drowning,
sinking,
falling,
suffocating

some days i will
float,
rise,
stand,
breathe

i will create
a boat of myself,

i will fight
to remain afloat,

i will eventually rise
back up when i don't,

and i will take a deep breath
before going under again

{ANXIETY ATTACK}

there is a dark shadow that hovers over me
most days i feel gloomy,
unmotivated,
unworthy
some days the sun comes out and starts to uncover me,
but it never lasts
because within the shadows
lie my flaws,
my weaknesses
the sunshine never seems
to reach them
i am stone cold,
unnoticed,
a thundered cloud

i am a thunderstorm

i do not rain; i pour
i do not water the land; i drown it
i am not the kind of storm you sit back and watch;
i am not the storm you chase;
i am not a summer night's storm,
where the air is warm and the raindrops kiss your skin;
i am the kind of storm that is catastrophic

{RATIONALIZING}

in the after storm
where i have reached equilibrium
with my surroundings,
there will be damage
and catastrophe
but there will also be light
and a rainbow that colors the sky
after the storm
is when i see the reality of things
i see the ones
who stayed to watch;
i hear the cries
of those who survived it with me;
i smell the rain
that kisses and heals;
and i feel the musty air
that has brought me back to life

{NEEDY}

i will plant the seeds
for my garden;
but water me when
i am weak and dry,
nurture me when
i get stepped on,
and show me
the sunshine,
so i don't have to take
the nutrients from those around me

{TO THE BONE}

while anxiety enjoys the buffet
of every last piece of my flesh

i am left raw;

starving to feel something

{MY THIRD TATTOO}

i have always tried
to look at life metaphorically
this makes it seem not so chaotic
and overwhelming
my metaphor for life is
balancing the sun and the moon
the sun being my strengths;
the moon being my weaknesses
i balance my weak points by creating,
creating to escape the darkness
that tries to consume me;
creating to be a light
for those who are also lost in the night
follow whatever light
draws you from your shadows,
and if you don't know what that light is,
follow me

{ENSLAVED}

i am
a slave of the past

sabotaged by
my own understanding
of love as a young child

from what i

saw,
heard,
and felt

{CURIOSITY}

this one is for the curious like me
because after all,
they are the ones who inspire me

the curious;

the ones who challenge themselves and their
ideas,
and do not ignore the curiosity that we all hold
within

they explore the things they do not know,
dig deeper into the things they already know,
and aspire to share for others to know

curiosity is what drives potential;
do not ignore it,
chase it

{DUAL MEANING OF SPACE}

space;
the place i go when anxiety takes over my body—outer
space, a vacant place. where there is not a sound but the
heavy breaths that pump out of my lungs. a place of zero
gravity; zero control. a feeling of nothing, and light as air.
as i float, flashbacks of who i am and why i am terrorize me,
having me wonder if i should even come back down

space;
the time between you and i; the time of being apart. although
this time seems to tick forever, it is the time we get to see
everything in its true form. we see the process, being the
progressions and retrogressions; what is working, and
what is destroying; our strengths, but also our weaknesses.
this time challenges us to trust, something never gained of
the past; this time challenges us to worry less, for we fear
the unknown; this time challenges us to accept, because
there are things we cannot control. this time between us
is a hard time, but a rewarding time. this time forces us to
trust time and space

// the balance in a relationship is time and space

{LIKE FATHER LIKE BOYFRIEND}

girls always date people like their father
they say

cheater,
manipulator,
liar

no wonder things
never last

{TOXIC RELATIONSHIPS}

oh,
the years wasted with you

not that i want the time back
but the life back

because i died a little inside
each and every time

{PERSPECTIVE}

everyone feels seasons a different way
because
a gloomy, winter day
means feeling the warmth of your arms
wrapped around me

// winter is my favorite season

{HEALING}

plants need a period of freezing
for future growth;
as do we

{INSECURITIES}

all my life
i have just wanted to be loved
the way that i love

but how foolish of me
to expect such a desired love
when i can't even give it to myself

// self-love, a broken concept of mine

{MY TWENTIETH BIRTHDAY}

it's been twenty years of being this composite of atoms
where they have been
both positive and negative;
both stable and unstable
on this continuous journey of self-love,
i have realized i am more than this chemical structure
that takes up space,
time,
and gravity

this twentieth year
i am going to focus on cleaning my conscience

like cleaning a bedroom,
i will organize one area at a time
i will first go through the precious things,
like going through an old jewelry box filled with
antiques passed down;
to remember where i am from
i will then move on to a drawer base
to refold some clothes;
to organize my thoughts and plans for the future
to finish off i will clean out the closet,
like cleaning out all the unwanted thoughts;
to create space for the new and better ones

// bring on the twenties

{LIFE IMITATES ART}

getting lost in the words
of your favorite book

losing all feeling
of your own emotions

pretending to feel the pain
not of your own,
but of the character's

until you realize
they are one in the same

// a contradiction of reading
to escape your own reality

{SUNDAY SCARIES}

should not be that scary at all
Sunday
the first day of the week,
the last day of the weekend
the day we dread because
tomorrow is another workday
but also,
the day we look forward to
because it is a day to
relax,
reflect,
recreate
recreating the week to be better
than the one before
and then the following week
better than this one
because after all,
every day of our life we are shedding a layer
one layer closer to the end of our time
so nourish the one underneath
that raw,
new layer
is a new beginning
another chance
to be better than the last,
until the very end

{STORYTELLING}

every time
that i find myself lost again

is when words find my lips
and my lips savor over the thought of you

and the thought of you
being no more finds my pen

and my pen finds my fingertips
that are no longer intertwining with yours

// broken love stories are what i write best

{THE AMERICAN DREAM}

(n). the ideal that every U.S. citizen should have an equal
opportunity to achieve success and prosperity through
hard work, determination, and initiative

but how is that so,
when we are building walls to keep the dreamers out?

{MY FIRST EX-LOVER}

depression is real
and shouldn't be taken as a joke at all

because while the sun is shining
they're still trying to hide

and for the one
who took my shadow as a joke
and laughed in my face

who is laughing now?

{HOUSE VS. HOME}

the problem with the girl
who grew up in a broken home
is she looks for a home
within a him
a him where she can unpack her things,
no longer living out of a duffle
but she forgets
the meaning of home
one of nurture
affection
love
she is looking to fill that vacancy
(the divorce)
of the hole in her chest
(her heart)
and fills it with a house
not a home

// know the difference

{NIGHTMARE OF A DAYDREAM}

most mornings
i do not want to get out of bed

most mornings
i would rather fall back asleep for an eternity,

where i can live in my nightmares
because at least those are not real

but living with this demon in my head
during my waking hours, is

{START WALKING}

every time you hurt me
is also every time you make me feel
stronger,
confident enough
to walk away

{BROKEN TRUST}

you are trying to build a new bridge
over the body of water filled with

lies,
bad habits,
broken promises

while i am still drowning with the old one
that our relationship was built on

// quit wasting your time, honey.
the damage has already been done

{NARCISSIST}

i don't know who you are anymore
or maybe i never knew
because all of your biggest,
darkest secrets
are now starting to come out

blinded by your charm,
i was
but what an alarm
when i finally asked myself,
what are you still doing here?

{2016}

she was still just a teen

when her English homework
became her works of art

and the aches and pain
became a huge part

of what her hands could create
with just pen and paper

// when words first saved me

{MISUNDERSTOOD}

why do you like taking pictures of the sky so much?
maybe it's because
rain or shine
it is always painted so beautifully
and different every time
or maybe it's because
i want to be a light to this world
and to be different from the rest
just like every sunset
and every sunrise;
different
or maybe it's in jealousy of the clouds
immune to gravity
floating carelessly into space
away from a world who does not understand me
who does not accept me
for feeling
a concept i still do not understand

// morning traffic jam thoughts
as i watch the sun, rise

{CHOICES}

some days she paints of greys and blues
some days she paints of yellows

you choose your hues

// choose yellow

{BE KIND}

coffee shops
a reminder that we are all here for similar reasons

to get shit done
to converse
to share smiles

or maybe,
to just get by

{UNFINISHED PROJECTS}

you shouldn't have to
paint him a different color
or hang up pictures on his walls
to make him feel like home
home is not an unfinished project
that will never get done,
it's a feeling

// do you feel at home?

{DEAD ENDS}

we have hit a dead end
once driving on smooth,
fresh pavement

while listening to our favorite songs
ones that cured our broken hearts,
piecing us back together

now we are listening to different songs
and left with nothing but a dirt road,
leading us to nowhere

{THE UGLY TRUTH}

lust is the last string
holding us together

and maybe a few other things, too
but all i know

is when we are making love,
is the only time i feel satisfied with you

{DISCOVERY OF MY VOICE}

my final class project was my therapy
and didn't really feel like homework at all
i was stuck in a trance,
humming my own words in my head
this is when my story began
the story of opening up,
accepting,
and realizing,
that i had a voice, too

// my first public journal in 2016

{FREE SPEECH}

i realized something
sitting quietly in that English class
doing a free writing activity
getting to write so freely
just me,
that piece of paper,
and pen
the issue with feeling everything so strongly
was not the issue itself
it was the people that made me feel
that feelings were not meant to be felt
nor shared
in the demeanor of expressing them so freely

// my professor freed me

{CAPTIVE}

he is not making me stay
but rather,
i am holding myself captive
because i am scared of freedom

what it looks like
what it feels like
to be alone,
for it has been so long

// set yourself free,
to love yourself first before him

{2010}

i was just ten years old
when i was split in half
left with nothing
but two broken halves of a heart
one half for myself to grip tight,
in hopes i had enough love left in me
to give away someday
the other half to choose a side
mom or dad?
i had to choose wisely
to get the love and affection
i so desperately desired through it all

// choosing sides,
an ongoing battle with divorced parents

{SELFLESS}

when we make love
you make sure we both finish

that's when i realized you
were different from the rest

{ANXIETY AND OCD}

divorce comes in twos
two roofs,
two rooms
something i could get used to
new town,
new school,
new house with new rules

freedom

a trap it was
to have to grow up too fast
while everyone else
was making memories to last
alone at night
because he was at a bar
to feel alright
scared,
so to others i ran
and this is where it all began

{DADDY ISSUES}

the first man you trust;
mine was filled with lust

i could never understand
why dad was touching women
other than my mother,
and then another

the habit hasn't died,
but i have inside

my heart is always breaking
for all the women aching

all because a man
with an addiction,
will stop nothing short
from getting his fixation

{TROPHY WIFE}

i don't want to be
just a part of your ego,
a metal of victory
because you won me over
or just that piece of art hung up
to look pretty for everyone to see
i want to be what we are
behind closed doors
undressed,
in love

// when he acts differently
around his friends

{NUMB}

resting bitch face
people say i have
with every emotion

happiness,
pain,
joy,
anger

all the same
displayed across my face
because it all feels the same

my cure
and how i know,
is there are infinite combinations of letters
making a surplus of words

that my one hand
and my one pen get to make art out of
indefinitely,
for a lifetime

and this is how i know
that this therapy
will never die,
and now neither will i

{GROW TOGETHER}

not one flame burns forever
if we do not feed this fire
we will be nothing
but the ashes we started at

// i always fall for the
broken ones

{SHINE YOUR LIGHT}

stop searching to be found

in a world of hate
and misunderstanding

the right people will find you
and bring you home

// those blinded by the world
cannot see the light anyway

{SLEEPLESS NIGHTS}

i am laying here,
awake
feeling sick
at the thought of you
and how you treat me
and you are pretending
to be asleep but
i know you can hear
every tear drop
and every sob
come out of my mouth
but do nothing

// that makes me
feel sicker

{USED AND ABUSED}

people who say they love you
at their own convenience
but when you're on the ground,
at your weakest
and they are fast asleep,
dreaming;
they are not in love with you

{WORKING OUT}

(lifting weights)
to imagine i am feeling all the aches
and all the pains
that have been placed amongst my backbone,
and releasing them

(running)
until i no longer feel that ache
and that pain
because it is after that,
that i feel numb

and feeling numb
feels better than the aches
and the pains,
that is why i sweat

// when i restarted my fitness journey in 2018

{GRATITUDE}

everything is temporary
both your pain
and your happiness

so do not dwell on your heartache
but also,
do not take your heartbeats for granted

{RAPE}

i bite my lips till they are raw,
an anxious habit of mine

it started after you
with me trying to rid the thought of you

and those lips
you so forcefully laid upon mine

as if you were some sort of animal
and i was your prey

// but you are no longer my predator

{BE STILL}

i took a bath for the first time in awhile
and as i lay here in calm waters
i am reminded of stillness
that everything has the capability of it

even in the natural disaster
of your own thoughts
you, too
have the power to be still

{MY BROWN-EYED LOVER}

it is those pool of honey eyes of yours
that drown me

so deeply in love,
so sweet

always wanting another taste

{BE YOUR OWN SUNSHINE}

it feels so good to be sun-kissed again
a kiss,
something i have to beg for from you
sunshine reminds me of how good it feels
to love yourself,
your skin,
your body
in the same way the sun loves you
it is the cloudy days
when i forget that feeling

{EATING DISORDERS}

commonly done by will
they say

but what about the disorder
where it is not a choice

to have the nerves of your stomach
eat at you from the inside out?

// self-diagnosis

{MAKE-UP}

what a concept,
it is

that we place this paint
(makeup)
onto an already beautiful, blank canvas
(our face)

and call it art

// there is nothing wrong with this
artistry. but make this art for yourself,
not for them

{MINE}

the way you arch your back
when we're making love

gliding my fingers down your spine;
a piece of mine

it's in this moment
that anxiety lets it be just you and i

no worries;
no insecurities

just you and i,
in love

{EMOTIONAL CHEATING}

(v). one partner channeling physical or emotional energy,
time, and attention into someone other than the person
they are in a committed relationship with to the point that
their partner feels neglected

 emotional cheating; the kind of cheating not talked about,
neglected, misinterpreted, taken as a joke. i could never
figure out why my heart was always aching at the sight, and
at the sound of attention being given to someone other than
me. there's no physical interaction being done, i thought,
until my counselor opened my eyes to this term commonly
unheard of. this term defined as channeling all your energy
into your partner, but not receiving the same in return.
stupid of me to have my body now comparing to hers in
jealously; something that never goes away. painful, it is, to
be looking at your partner in awe while he is looking at her

// let us change the stigma, because this kind of
cheating hurts just as bad. how is you and your partner's
connection? is he looking at you, or her?

{HOME AT LAST}

i am an artist,
and this is my gallery

artist;
not defined as it once was

it now serves as anything creative
and everything in between;

it's acknowledging your feelings
and voicing them in your own way;

it's creating the vision that not everyone
has the capability of seeing

my artistry is the releasing of words that
chime in my head,
day in and day out

i now feel that i have a place
where i belong

to my fellow artists,
i am happy to be home

{I AM THE MOON}

i wonder what the moon says to the sun at dawn
is the moon jealous of the sun?
jealous of the light it gets to shine
the attention it receives at daytime
when everyone is awake
when everyone is alive
because when the moon shines,
everyone is asleep

i feel like the moon

i glow
and i shine
while everyone is
dreaming their own dreams
thinking their own thoughts
and it is at dusk,
that i fall behind the shadows once again

// i shine the brightest
in the darkness

{BACKSTABBERS}

do not be mistaken by a dull blade,
it is more likely to cut you than a sharp one

// choose your blade wisely

{MY SECRET WEAPON}

how do you write so easily?
so beautifully?

i have been through a lot of heartache
and pain that peeled,
that peeled layers of life off of me

and this is the only remedy
that has healed,
that has healed every raw layer

until i feel
reborn again,
and then i try again

// my writing does not come easy.
it comes from
the hurt,
the ache,
the pain

{STOMACHACHE}

you are the knot in my stomach
that never seems to go away

{MUSIC IS A LOVE LANGUAGE}

when you can listen to the same songs again,
that's when you know you are over them

{LOVE IS LOVE}

we accept tree-huggers;
humans loving trees

but we do not accept lgbtq+;
humans loving humans

{OVER-THINKING}

a curse it is
to be stuck in my head all day,
always humming a sad love song

{THE HEART OF A VIRGO}

i channel so much of my energy
into other people

i give,
and give,
and give

they take,
and take,
and take

i guess that's just
the Virgo in me

// us Virgos
are not compatible
with anyone

{A POOR EXCUSE FOR RAPE CULTURE}

when we wear revealing clothes
we are asking for our flesh to be eaten
at the bone by the beasts,
the beasts of human nature; men

// how can we tame the beasts?

{NUDE}

when we undress for him,
we are praised

when we undress for ourselves,
we are crucified

// the modern crucifixion
of the female

{DEPRESSION}

i used to think of myself as seasons,
but seasons change
and i have not

// i want to be winter
going on spring

{THE SHORT TALE OF A WRITER}

i write these words
that are written,

because the thoughts my heart speaks
cannot be spoken

{RACISM}

hating your neighbor
for being painted a different color than you

is like hating an artist
for the choice in color of their painting

// God is the artist and we are the canvas.
dare to still critique?

{FOREIGN LANGUAGE}

writing,
my fluent language

but a language barrier to many

{VERBAL ABUSE}

my words cut deep,
but so did the ones that brought me here

{LOVE-HATE RELATIONSHIPS}

the most painful thing,
i think

is to hate someone
as much as you love them

{FORGIVENESS}

Spring is the forgiveness of Winter
that we so desperately desire every year

where the flowers still bloom
despite the cold that sucked them dry,
abandoned to freeze for three long months

if only human nature could act upon one another
as nature itself does

this would be a place of
balance,
beauty,
peace

{MOTHER NATURE KNOWS BEST}

seasons change,
and so should humanity

{CLINGY}

distance scares me
because the time between you and i
leaves me thinking

stuck in my thoughts of the
what,
who,
how,
why
of every possibility

time apart
feels like an eternity,
a long-distance relationship

because all we have ever known
is sucking the life out of each other

this habit of ours is killing me inside,
because the attachment has been made

{LUST}

i undress for you as fast as
flowers do come Spring

{LOST}

when your weaknesses
become his triumphs

you lose more than just
his silly little game

// you lose yourself, too

{EMPTY}

how can you give energy
to something,
or someone

who has already drained it
all out of you?

you can't give
what you don't have

{A WRITER'S MISCHIEF}

i think to myself
how nice it would feel
to be alone

but then i wouldn't feel
the heartbreaks,
the tears,
the cries

or the happiness,
the laughs,
the love

they always think they played me,
used me,
like a cheap piece of art

but look at what
i have created of them

// i used them

{FIND YOUR PASSIONS}

everything happens for a reason,
but nothing will happen without reason

{ROBBED}

i gave you the spare key to my padlock
(my heart)

to be my security,
but you lost the key a long time ago

no wonder i feel stripped
of everything good and rich i once held

// be your own security

{PRESENCE}

time is supernatural,
where days seem longer in the given moment
and

months,
years,
decades,
centuries

seem shorter
because all the todays catch up eventually,
and all of those todays are what turn into the

months,
years,
decades,
centuries

in a blink of an eye

// how are you spending your time today?

{A TICKING TIME BOMB}

space between two mortals in love
can be the best thing,
or the worst thing;
the time can be revered
and heal,
or the time can be abused
and oppress

// time will tell

{YOUR CHOICE}

mental illness is like a shadow;
it will always be there

but you choose whether to be afraid of it,
or to accept it as a part of you

{INDUSTRIALIZATION}

hold onto the ones
who make time stand still

we live in a society
that does not

{MEMORIES}

moments do not last forever,
but the feelings do

you choose how the time is spent;
spend it well

{GROW WITH THEM OR BE OUTGROWN}

be humble to the ones you outgrow,
and confident enough to let them go

be supportive to the ones who have outgrown you,
and wise enough to know that it is your season, too

{BE CAREFUL WHO YOU BURN}

when we are at peace,
we set fire to souls

when we are at war,
we set fire to cities

but how foolish of us to believe
that we can control what our fire chooses to burn

{TRUTH HURTS}

some nights,
we talk for hours
some nights,
we do not speak at all

but the sad thing is
silence speaks louder
than the soft words before bed
that we sometimes give

because when we go from
tangled up in the sheets
to tangled up in our twisted minds,
is when all the truths come out

// silence, our enemy

{BODY OVER MIND}

a message to the over-thinkers like me:

when you heart starts speaking to you
louder than your mind,
listen to it

{SEX}

our love can only be found
tangled up in the bedsheets

so that is where i go,

to get the only kind of love
i believe i deserve

{LOVE YOURSELF FIRST}

when a honeybee comes across a bud of a flower
it flirts and pecks
and the bud smiles and tries to force growth
but Mother Nature demands time
time to grow naturally
to grow slowly
as for us, too
we must have time
to heal
to bud
to nourish
to grow
to bloom
in order to give all of our love to that sweet honeybee,
someday

no wonder everything in nature is so beautiful come
Springtime
they simply take three whole months
to heal
to bud
to nourish
to grow
to bloom
because you can't give your all to someone
until you have done it for yourself,
first

{INTROVERTED}

i write
to be understood

because the words that roll off my tongue
never could

// an introvert, but not by choice

{STRANGERS}

i envy the ones who can look at you,
and still see all the good

when i look at you,
all i see is the evil

and this pain you've brought me to;
here is to the man i once knew

{FALL LIKE THE SNOW}

the snow is falling
and we should be falling with it;
falling madly in love with
someone,
someplace,
something

// we need to live lovingly,
to live fully

{SCARED OF MY OWN SHADOW}

i glow brighter apart from you;
maybe you were the shadow that had me scared
to be anything and everything
i wanted to be

{KNOW YOUR WORTH}

you get so concerned
when others give me

the attention,
the support,
the gratitude,

that i deserve;
maybe because you never could

{HEART-BREAKER}

be cautious of the ones
with a pretty face
and a broken heart

{SELFISH}

have you ever dated someone,
where you're staring at him
while he's staring at the mirror?

{SWEET DREAMS}

all of the silent,
lonely nights
tucked away
in those cold bed sheets
without you
while you were out doing
a bad habit
you couldn't control

but tonight

is the first time
that i feel in control
with myself
warm in these bed sheets
still tucked away
but content,
and dreaming a happy dream

{SELF-CARE}

in all reality
we never stop healing

we just get to a point
where it no longer feels like a job,
but rather a habit

to do the things for ourselves
that we should've been doing all along

{PEOPLE CHANGE}

you used to be a real peach
but peaches rot
and so do people

{PLOT TWIST}

you were the first to show me
that i can write of happy love stories, too

remind me of this,

so our ending can be rewritten
as our new beginning

{CONSENT}

body language
speaks louder than words
the way he stares
as your clothes drop to the floor

// are your bodies speaking
the same language?

{OPEN MIND}

soft spoken
does not always mean close minded,
because the softest spoken
are often the most open minded

{WORLD HUNGER}

we are all suffering from it
some for food,
some for peace of mind

it is the ones not starving for
more money,
more things

and the ones not hungry for
the opinions of others,
nor the validation

that are the fullest;
because they are self-fed

// we are all starving in this
world, and not just
for food

{RE-BIRTH}

like a flower

you are planting,
you are growing,
you sprout

then you become frail,
you wilt,
and maybe die a little inside

but the cycles of nature
always repeat
and so can ours

Mother Nature has designed these cycles
so beautifully,
so perfectly

that even after the plant dies
it has already produced self-sustaining
offsets that surround

which means
not the end,
but a new beginning

{KEEP GROWING}

honey,
don't waste your time
on the one
who only chooses to pick
the live flowers
and never the growing
ones

{NATURAL DISASTERS}

i'm dependent

i need you like an ocean does water
and a forest does trees;

no wonder people drown
and forests burn

{MIXED EMOTIONS}

you feel like rain
and sunshine,
all at once

{TAKE YOUR TIME}

sometimes we just grow apart
and often at different paces

in our friendships,
relationships,
acquaintances

but in nature
that never makes one flower
prettier than the one
growing more slowly

keep growing,
keep loving

no matter how long it takes,
the process is beautiful

{FAKE LOVE}

so often today
we try to conform to our partner
or mold our partner to be a clone of ourselves
and call it love

{FALSE HOPE}

i am in love with the idea
of what we could have been,
but that is not enough for
the enemies we have become

{OUT OF BREATH}

maybe we are just too far gone
and not worth chasing

{ALCOHOLIC}

never again
will i take a sip of whiskey,
it tastes like you

{REALIZATIONS}

spending time
without you
made me realize
i am better off
without you

{CRY, BABY, CRY}

when the sky cries of rain,
the flowers celebrate

when we cry,
they label us weak

{KEEP DREAMING}

have you ever thought
that maybe,

just maybe,

the galaxy up above is
a dreamscape

and the night sky is
the dream catcher

that holds the billions
of dreams in the
shapes of stars?

if so,

our dreams
are not going anywhere,

until the night that the
moon decides to
burn out

{BE PRESENT}

all we ever really have
is this exact moment

the past
has passed

the future
is out of reach

{WHY I WRITE}

for the ones
scared
to openly tell the
truth of their
feelings,
heartaches,
anything
and everything
through vulnerability

{MAKE-UP SEX}

the make-up sex
is worth all the heartbreaks
from you

{LOVE LOST IN MEMORIES}

our love was left behind in Minnesota;
the last good memory we have

just as the sun
rises in the east
and
sets in the west,

we, too

can
rise on one side
of the earth
and
set on the other

do not waste the light
of the sun
and
of the moon

{HEALTHY CHOICES}

if it doesn't feed you,
why even allow it on your plate?

{CO-DEPENDENCY}

i went to take a drink
out of my glass
only to realize i emptied
it all into yours
making mine not half full
nor half empty,
just empty

{IMBALANCE}

i give
you take

i break

...

{TURN YOUR HEARTBREAKS INTO ART}

you've hurt me in ways
i can't undo

hurt, so bad

that i will continue writing
poems about you

every time my heart breaks
and shatters into a million pieces,
my art begins to pick up the pieces
and prepares me for something better
and even more beautiful than the last

heartbreaks do not get easier,
but they do make you
stronger and wiser
of what you deserve

this story ends with heartbreak
because realistically
there are no happy endings,
just peace

for the past thirty-six months
i had been living in my dreams,
in a trance
i felt like i was not even living
nor alive at all
but rather taking up useless space
my priorities shifted,
my dreams were fading
until i woke up
with all of my words
and all of my love
in my very own book
sometimes you have to live
in your daydreams for a little while,
that's how dreams come true

i hope this book leaves you feeling the power that is within
each and every one of you. the power to release the knots
amongst your backbone, and to plant seeds in its place.
once you can release of the things causing those aches and
pains, the planting grounds become endless

// keep planting

healing is constant,
healing is growth,
healing is only the beginning

www.ingramcontent.com/pod-product-compliance
Lightning Source LLC
Chambersburg PA
CBHW032025050726
47590CB00006B/2305